The Illegible Bachelor

By the same author

I Hank Marvinned . . .
Essex Festival, 1991

Under Milk Float
with wood engravings by Barry Woodcock
The Greyhound Press, 1992

Both books are available through

Festival Books
The Essex Festival
University of Essex
Wivenhoe Park
COLCHESTER
Essex
CO4 3SQ

The Illegible Bachelor

Martin Newell

Festival Books
from The Greyhound

First published in Great Britain
by Festival Books
Reprinted 1996

ISBN 0 9519100 5 1

Cover design by Richard Stokes
Cover photograph of Martin and Terry by Denise Turner
Typography by Agnesi Text Hadleigh Suffolk
Printed by Progressive Printing Leigh on Sea Essex

Festival Books (from The Greyhound)
is an imprint of The Essex Festival Colchester Essex CO4 3SQ

To 'The Kid'

Thanks to

Joe Allard for editing . . .
Denise Turner for the photo . . .
Captain Sensible for the blurb . . .

and

Wunderbarmaid

Contents

Ah hello then reader

Here's a motley collection of my poetry, tour diaries and other bits and bobs. It's taken me over three years to amass this much stuff. This is largely because, again, my attention was distracted by the siren call of the music biz. I've made two full-length CDs since I wrote *Under Milk Float*. In addition to this, a lot of my old records got re-released. I'm scampering around in my forties now and have grave doubts as to whether making pop records is a good idea or not. Poetry is a much gentler mistress than the harsh dominatrix of rock music.

I've been abroad a lot in the past three years. Fragments from diaries herein will attest to this. It was interesting but I'd still rather be in Wivenhoe woods, throwing sticks for the dog. It's strange to find that if you get stuff published as a writer you're legit. If you get stuff released as a musician, even if it's well reviewed and sells respectably, you're worthless unless you've got some money.

One way or another, age and an association with literature have led to my almost MacVicaresque rehabilitation into polite society. I go into schools now to talk about poetry. A few years ago if they saw people like me near schools they got on the radio for back-up from the TSG.

So why does anyone parade their daubing, scrawlings or warblings in front of a largely sceptical public? Well, about half of it's creative burning, I reckon. The other half is definitely a case of 'Mummy, you're not watching me.'

But the performer needs a bit of approval. Like Tinkerbell in *Peter Pan*. If not enough children clap their hands, she dies.

I hope you like some or all of the stuff in this, my third volume. I work on it and I'm trying to refine it too. So clap your hands or the fairy gets it.

Your man in Essex

September 1995

Planet Newell
Wivenhoe
Essex

The Last Boys in the Wood

August, tinder dry
The woods belong to me
The wind, the magpies, and the lazy sun
And all the boys have grown up and are gone
John, three years away
And Will on soldier's pay
And Steven building boats in Brightlingsea
And Simon, lost his mind to LSD.

The kids no longer come
Cos fearful Dad or Mum
Reminded by the news of violent ends
Now chauffeur them by car to visit friends
No boyish voices ring
No camping kettles sing
The treehouse Simon built when he was well
Is long abandoned now, an empty shell.

All these lads were good
The last boys in the wood
I listen for the voices, there are none.
Just me, the wind, the magpies
Me, the wind, the magpies
Me, the wind, the magpies and the sun
And all the sacred innocence is gone.

The Stupidity Tax (Instants of Stupidity)

'Ten quid a week I put aside
The kids need shoes
The rabbit died
He never had his Mixy jabs
Gissa coupla Instants, Babs.'

On Saturday at eight or so
The streets gone quiet, the TV on
The greedy glint in people's eyes
With dreams of cars and holidays
And furniture and gadgetry
And indolence and cushy times
Of sun-burned leisure, lounging round
For ever in some vulgar house
With leaded lights and swimming pool
A cocktail-shaker handy by
And all the steaks a fridge can hold
And private health care when they're old.
And horses for the girls to ride
And Go-Karts for the boys to drive
And everything on video
The future in a rosy glow.

Soft focus through the mirror then
To win that cash – Not if but *when*.
'And *we* will never change,' they vow.
But best go into hiding now . . .

And somewhere in another place
A suited handshake, beaming face
The politician and his spouse
Award themselves an opera house.

I have not paid my Stupidity Tax
I will not pay my Stupidity Tax
I will NEVER pay my Stupidity Tax

Go on.
Gissa coupla Instants then.

Grandad

I decided to name the baby
After my grandfather
So we called it 'Grandad'.
Got no thanks for it.
She's nineteen now.

Goldilocks on Different Types of Drugs

Acid

And then Baby Bear said,
'Who's been sleeping in my porridge?

Whizz

'We used to have some chairs they were exactly like
that well a bit like that my mum got them from MFI
I think it was in the new year sales anyway at the time
we had this new cat and it managed to crawl under the
wardrobe and hey you haven't got any chocolate have
you and I'm really thirsty shall I go out and buy some
cigarettes I've only got forty left . . .'

Heroin

'Oh wow . . . right . . . you're back. Yeah hey look.
Like I'm really sorry but I had to sell the beds and the
chairs while you were out. I'm sorry about the works
on the table and the blood in the porridge and that.
But like . . . I'm getting off soon. Really. The clinic
said I'll be down to drinking methadone by next
month . . .'

Guardian Personals w.l.t.m.

He
Would like to meet
A woman who
Likes theatre/walking
Films and art
Leftish/bookish/veggie/slim
Wants to spend her life with him
London or South East might do
But . . . Oh God he needs a screw.

She
Is tall, professional,
Strawberry-blonde
Wants to form a lasting bond
With an easy-going guy
Mustn't be afraid to cry
Sense of humour, going out
Thirty-something thereabouts
Likes the Clash and Billy Bragg
And . . . She's gasping for a shag.

But
Knobs and fannies, tits and tongues
Thrusting loins and heaving lungs
Never mind his swollen tum
Or her great gargantuan bum
This is what you wanted. Do it.
Get your kit off and get to it.
Slap and tickle, scratch and prickle
Up Ben Nevis, down the crevice
Broomstick rigid, juices flowing
Engines purring, faces glowing
In and out and in and out

Up and down and up and down
Don't forget to swivel round
Grind the pubis through the ground
Go and go and go and go
Don't pretend it isn't so
Half the adverts in the rag
Should really read, 'I NEED A SHAG.'

Proverb from London SE8

In the midst of life,
We are in Deptford.

Blond Erudition

In July–August of 1994 I went to Iceland as a guest of Jakob Frímann Magnússon, who was cultural attaché at the London Embassy at that time. I did several poetry performances and a handful of interviews. I spent much of my time in Reykjavík but also visited Thingvellir, a place of supernatural beauty and site of the Althing, Iceland's original ancient parliament. In the middle of my stay I was asked by Jakob if I would like to visit Akureyri, a town three hundred miles to the north. In early August we took the ferry from Reykjavík to Akranes and from there, drove in an old red Chevrolet for six hours through a sort of permanent twilight to our destination. During this journey, some of it on roads not much more than mountain tracks, I saw some of the most alien landscape I've ever experienced. The following passages however, are culled from my tour diary and mostly take in my time spent in Reykjavík. Much of this diary was published in the Independent *on 25 August 1994.*

I get into Reykjavík at 3.30 a.m. just as it's getting dark. At 3.45 a.m. it starts getting light again. That's the kind of wild nutty place that Reykjavík is. It's the eve of the biggest bank holiday of the year, it's wet, it's 55°F. and most young Icelanders are being rained on at festivals. In Iceland, summers are so wet that you go to a festival equipped *as* a condom rather than *with* one.

There are fourteen recording studios in Reykjavík but only three liquor stores. A sort of numb disbelief settles upon this touring poet. 'Don't worry, Martin,' says Dora, my hostess. 'We'll sort something out.' Bibulous locals stock up well in advance.

My first performance is in a large disco. In the wash-room, prior to my performance, I'm accosted by a

6ft 5ins crop-haired bouncer. He shakes my hand and says, 'I'm really looking forward to your set, I'm a big poetry fan.' Relieved and incredulous I reply, 'Yes, you are.'

There are about 265,000 Icelanders, descended from Norwegian, Hebridean and Irish Vikings who arrived some thousand years ago. They clearly didn't let anybody ugly on the longships. People here are enviably tall, clean-limbed and good-looking. They also buy more books and records *per capita* than any other nation on earth and are intimidatingly well educated. They formed the world's first parliament or Althing in AD 930 and haven't looked back since.

Two days after my first performance I see the modern parliament house in Reykjavík. An imposingly small building, it has less apparent security than an allotment shed. Anyone with the airfare and a small family selection box of Brock's Fireworks could cause a major international incident here. But nobody hates the Icelanders. The only people who ever went to war with them were us. And we lost.

The biggest rock band to come out of Iceland were Stuthmenn. Jakob Frímann Magnússon was keyboard player with Stuthmenn prior to defecting to the diplomatic service. In the 1980s, Stuthmenn walked on water. A handy thing to be able to do in Iceland. They toured China with Wham in 1984 and sold an awful lot of records. They also made Iceland's biggest-grossing film ever. I saw it on video without the benefit of subtitles. It seemed to be somewhere between *A Hard Day's Night* and a punkish *Summer Holiday*.

Compared to Stuthmenn, The Sugarcubes were rank outsiders who eventually fared much better abroad. Pictures of one-time Sugarcubes singer Björk are to be seen everywhere although she now lives mostly in London. It's still possible to meet Einar or Thor from her earlier band in Reykjavík bars. Einar won't be drawn on the success of his colleague, but Dora my hostess, who's known her since Björk was nine, describes her as 'a nice kid'. Reading between the lines I surmise that Iceland is quietly but fiercely proud of Björk.

My poetry performances go down unexpectedly well. In general, the Icelanders' command of English is slightly better than our own. Not only do audiences understand the humorous poems, they laugh at the joke I stole that ends, 'No. You're doing that. I'm setting fire to the shed.'

Crime is so low in Iceland that a stabbing made second item on the national TV news. A young man had stabbed himself with a filleting knife while working. I'm also struck by how clean and energy-efficient this country is. All hot water comes from naturally heated volcanic sources and the electricity is from hydro-generators.

On my penultimate night here, four of us perform poetry in relay at four of Iceland's busiest pub/cafés. My three fellow poets are Sjón Sigurdsson, Linda Vilhjálmsdóttir and Elisabet Jökulsdóttir. They've never done this before but the Poetry Pub Crawl goes down a storm. Linda asks me about England. 'When they hear the word "poetry" where I live,' I reply, 'They generally reach for their dictionaries.'

By 3 a.m. on Friday, Young Iceland has decided that it's absolutely mad and it just doesn't care *what* it does. The whole square beneath my window has, in *Viz*-speak, gone completely hatstand. Hundreds of young people are roaring, trousers-down drunk. One chap, trying to weave out of the square on a bicycle, successfully falls off head first into a bush. In spite of the noise level, however, there's no outright vandalism or serious fighting. This is, apparently, an average Friday night in Reykjavík, even if the roar from the square below sounds like a poll-tax riot. 'They're just having one hell of a party,' Jakob Frímann Magnússon assures me.

Appropriately enough, the last sign I read before leaving Keflavík airport the following Sunday is above an appeal box. It says: 'Leave your tree in Iceland.'

Vikings

In the murmur of a northern pub
A southern seagull blown off-course
I listen to the pack-dog wind
As, roaring drunk, the hooligan North Sea
Bawls the names of men who spoke in Norse
Men who saw these cliffs from longboat prow
Strangers then as I am now

And on this coat-piled bench, I sit and watch
A man unloading seacoal on stone flags
Talking to a woman in low tones
As she puts the coal in paper cones
To glow upon the fire and all this time
The bony ghosts of Vikings cluster round
Men who settled down and learned to plough
Strangers then as I am now.

Written in Saltburn, Cleveland, February 1993

In Autumn Attic

Autumn came to Wivenhoe and slowly
Turned to ash the opal of the sky
Lovers took the last train out of Clacton
Drunken insects zigzagged home to die.

Dutiful, the widow of the summer
Drifted through the apple-scented halls
This year's girl-most-likely-to was hanging
Rusty leaves on musty redbrick walls.

Westerlies, the stagehands of the season,
Moved to shift the scenery away
Ruffled up the river down to Rowhedge
Drew the evening in to close the day.

Somewhere through the trees, a train to London
Sparked the overheads and slid from sight
Deeper in the woods a dog was barking
Someone on the station said goodnight.

Huddled in the pub the early drinkers
Turned to see the window spanked by rain
Not to hear the calling of the curlew
Nor the ghosts of children in the lane.

Passport to Rowhedge

They're foreigners in Rowhedge
Their ways are not like ours
Their houses hunch in little lanes
They have no access to the trains
The fact that there's no bridge explains
The way they are in Rowhedge.

They're very strange in Rowhedge
They keep it to themselves
The reasons why the streets are quiet
And secrecy's the local diet
You're hardly going to get a riot
They way they are in Rowhedge.

But when the final ferry's gone
There's something sinister goes on
The lonely hooting of an owl
A frightened dog begins to howl
The secret police are on the prowl
And if you stay in Rowhedge . . .
Beware the footsteps in the street
The marching of official feet
You see that big eight-sided steeple?
That's where they imprison people.
Others who've been caught alone
End up face down in the Colne
This is not the Twilight Zone
Stranger still, it's Rowhedge.

And when you catch the ferry
The tillerman might say,
　'Make sure that you're here by four
　One last trip and then no more
　Don't know what may be in store
　If you're stuck in Rowhedge.'

And passports should be valid
And permits must be stamped
Bikes and dogs included
Even if it's cramped

Or you'll be stuck in Rowhedge
And God knows what you'll do
The embassy can't help you then
There's no escape and who knows when
Or *if* you'll see your home again
They're foreigners in Rowhedge . . .

Horses Seen Through Trees

For Terry O'Connell

Some silver autumn morning
Remember days like these
As horses seen through trees.

And in forgotten orchards
The ochre of the sun
And echo of a gun.

A gale bends the birches
The elders crick and groan
The moon is smashed to pieces
In waters of the Colne
And autumn drags you home.

The dead are reacquainted
With living they have known
Their half-remembered faces
In flowers, moss and stone.
Ashes, earth or bone.

And if I die in early autumn,
Light a fire, boy – in the woods.
Build it well and crack a bottle.
Share out all my worldly goods.

And on some silver morning
Remember days like these
As horses seen through trees.

Introduction to *A Child's Christmas in Essex*

In Search of Ted Jarvis *by Martin Newell, with a foreword by Sybil Hedingham, will be published by Long & Melford in early 1997. Price £141.95.*

Ted Jarvis was a rustic poet and homespun philosopher from the village of Wivenhoe in north-east Essex. He disappeared in 1990 leaving a few scrawled notebooks of his poems and thoughts. His story is recounted mainly by the people who knew him and I have collated much of this information as the basis for a forthcoming book.

Ted's main mentor was the writer Sybil Hedingham, author of *The Heart is a Lonely Tiger*, *A Foreigner Abroad* and the blockbuster classic, *A Far Cry from Witham.* With her assistance I have chosen an earlier piece of Ted's writing to include in this, my own book. Hopefully it will help to bring to the attention of the public a rustic and original talent which I feel is every bit as important as that of John Clare or Robert Burns.

In *A Child's Christmas in Essex,* Ted writes about his childhood in his own East Anglian tongue and rhythm. Ted was the only child of a shopkeeper and a farm labourer and was very much out of step with his time. During the early 1960s when Ted was a young man, his village was subject to immense change. This was as a result of the building of Essex University a mile or so away from his home. This led to and coincided with the arrival of a large group of artists and writers to his previously quiet village.

In common with many poets, Ted Jarvis felt that the world he knew was rapidly disappearing. He had a burning urge to get it down on paper before it was lost for ever. Ted Jarvis was insular, selectively racist and homophobic. He was resentful of change and of those whom he saw as being responsible for it. In spite of this, he was suspicious of and clinically violent to the rather Bohemian newcomers to his village. *A Child's Christmas in Essex* is a good introduction to his work.

A Child's Christmas in Essex

Excerpt from In Search of Ted Jarvis

Sometimes that was sunny and sometimes that rained. It hardly ever snowed but if it did, that didn't last fer long cos the council gritters'd be out throwing salt and grit onter it t'make sure that didn't set in.

Sometimes that was just sorta grey and that always seemed like Sundy cos there was no shops and no traffic.

Me Dad ud be the first one up, burn'n all the Christmas wrappin paper and the trees which me Mum hadn't bin able t'sell. Then he'd come up t'me room and say, 'Wake up, Ted – that's toime fer yer Christmas beat'n.'

Some years, he'd wrap a piece o' tinsel round the stick he beat me with and other times he'd have a special Christmas stick made out of holly wood. That used t'hurt but that was very Christmassy.

After we'd had a bit o' breakfast, Mum ud say, 'Well, we moight as well all jist sit here, cos that's Christmas Day and we dun't have ter do n'work.'

Sometimes me Dad ud switch the wireless on and we'd all listen to the Hawaiian Guitar Serenaders doin'

Christmas carols from St Mary's, Colchester.

We usually had a turkey or two runnin' about the back yard behind the shop and me Mum and Dad ud have a traditional argument over who was gunna kill it. In the end, that ud be killed, plucked and put in the oven and me Mum ud give the innards t' the dog – which usually made that sick about mid-afternoon.

Dad ud make his Christmas walk over ter Brightlingsea straight after dinner. That was traditional. It always put Mum in a bad mood cos he didn't come back till Boxin' Day night. And I once heard her say, after he slammed out, 'I hope he catches someth'n.' But I didn't see how he could. Cos he never took his fish'n rod with him.

After that, Mum and me ud jist sit there till that got dark. There didn't seem n'point in doin' anythin' cos there never was.

On Boxin' Day, Monty Thorogood and Ernie Catchpole would come round and we'd go out look'n fer cats t'boot. Monty was best at it. He'd be able to disable a cat with one shot but that usually took me a couple or three gos. Then after that we'd go home and burn all the decorations, ready t'start gett'n things back t'normal again. I remember me Mum used t'say as the last paper chain crumbled to ash on Boxin' Day night, 'And a bloomin' good job too.' Cos that was two days takin's she'd lost through that y'see. After that, Dad ud stagger in, usually in a good mood, with his breath smellin' o' whisky and his flies undone. Then he'd wash his privates in an old pudd'n basin in front of the fire, sluice the dog sick in the back yard down the drain with the water from the bowl and say, 'Oi'm off t'bed, Dot – I'll beat Ted in the morn'n.'

And that was like that every Christmas fer years.

Portrait of Aretha

In black and white
With cigarette

In tight bouffant
With polo neck

And by piano
Sitting down

The concentration
In her frown

Her painted eyes
Her wedding band

Amerika
In palm of hand

Paradiddle Flam

For drummers everywhere

Paradiddle flam
Paradiddle flam
Anchor of a band
Bam Bam Bam
Mumma-dadda-mumma
I became a drummer
Practised in a shed
Stifling in summer
Never went to college
Didn't have the knowledge
Lumbered with an IQ
Still in double figures

Paradiddle flam
Paradiddle flam
I can tell a cymbal
From a lump of spam
Blap Blap Blap
Never took to Rap
Wouldn't catch me dead in
Trainers and a cap
Maybe I could settle
Playing heavy metal

Mumma-dadda-mumma
Happy as a drummer
Useless at discussion
Better at percussion
Tried to do a crossword
Seemed to be in Russian
Question number six
Had me in a fix

D blank blank M
'Instrument for sticks?'
Knew I couldn't win
Bunged it in the bin
Drummer's what I am
Paradiddle flam.

Roy Wood

Roy Wood
Was frighteningly good
But my past loyalties
Won't make him royalties.
I doubt if that's concerning 'em
Where he lives (in Birmingham).

What Did Your Last Servant Die Of?

What did your last servant die of?
Was it the drink or the drugs?
Was it from scrubbing the telltale stains
Out of the sheepskin rugs?
Was it from hauling you on to your bed
Everytime you were plastered?
No. It was multiple orgasms.
And get it right, you bastard.

Tom Waits for No Man

How would the lyrics of Tom Waits have been affected
if he'd come from Colchester?

You can't get any bagels
The coffee tastes of moss
There's no such thing as Satan
Just God being slightly cross
There's toothmarks on the Flymo
And Harpic in my beer
And Harry Secombe's wardrobe
Was launched and modelled here
A burned-out Datsun Cherry
Is smokin' in the street
Some Mucron on the dashboard
A crossbow on the seat
The shops are World of Darren
And Combat Boots R Us
Potato-U-Relate-To
While-Waiting-4-A-Bus

You wanna see excitement?
Let's hop a bus to town
It's over twenny years now
Since Woolworth's got burned down
And people wait here weekends
Around the Hippodrome
To beat up Blur's lead singer
And let him know he's home
So putcha cap on backwards
And tracksuit bottoms on
We'll go out to an Indian
And fight a man called Ron
Then home by blue-light taxi
For several hours' wait

To wire yer jaws together
And fit yer steel plate.

This town ain't got a graveyard
They don't cremate their dead
They sit them on the council
And leave them there instead
So cutcha hair by strimmer
But don't repaint your bike
They dunno much 'bout art here
But they know what they don't like.

First published in the Independent, *24 March 1994*

Cowboy of the County

Ah'm proud t'be a wrangler from East Anglia
Where real men still crah intew their beer
Great Yarmouth down t'Maldon
North-west t'Saffron Waldon
Them cowboys never hung their guns up here.
Jest went intew construction
Or clearing drains bah suction
They walk away from rubble if they can
Then take the cash and use it
On maudlin country music
Or tahger-skin acrylics for their van.

First published in the Independent, *1993*

There Goes Non-Rhyming Garfunkel

Awkward on the record sleeves
Haircut wasn't right
Candyfloss-on-rugby-ball
Not a pretty sight
Known for singing very high
Caught the acting habit
Followed by a solo smash
Song about a rabbit.
Here a brief reunion
There a brand new start
Some reviewers say it's pop.
Ah. But is it Art?

First published on the pop page of the Independent, *Christmas 1993*

Linda McCartney's Pies

Paul McCartney in the kitchen
Helping Linda with her pies,
Looked up from a finished pie-top
Gazed into his partner's eyes
Saying, 'Since the Beatles finished,
Critics claim my tunes are limper.
Is this how my world has ended?
Not with a twang but a crimper?'

First published on the pop page of the Independent,
Christmas 1993

Noddy Holder's Sacred Hat

By Noddy Holder's sacred hat
In mirror discs adorning that
The platform boots, the gaudy checks
The ruddy roughened cheeks convex
And mutton-chopped from ear to chin
In cheery Midland rustic grin

Nostalgia in the beery glow
Of Christmas twenty years ago
And once you'd heard, you understood
That nothing else could be as good
The brimstone larynx of the devil
On the boy they christened Neville.

First published on the pop page of the Independent,
Christmas 1993

John Cooper Clarke

John Cooper Clarke
Lives in the dark
And won't emerge
Till well gone three
Unlike Attila
Unlike me
His accent
Indicates the north
He leaves it late
To sally forth
With pointy boots
And skinny suits

Vacates his lair
With back-combed hair
A plastic bag
And purloined fag
His aching dental cavity
The wages of depravity

John Cooper Clarke
Nocturnal, stark
You'll never meet him
In the park
But if you really
Wish to see him
Try a stylish mausoleum

Dear Poetry Society

In 1994, the Poetry Society declared that poetry was, wait
for it, the New Rock 'n' Roll. *Suddenly, after years in the
dark, poetry was dragged out of its musty garrett, squeezed
into its stage clothes and shoved uncomprehending and
squinting into the light. Poetry then found itself on BBC
Radio One, on television and as the subject of numerous
articles in newspapers and magazines. It was announced that
there would be a National Poetry Day.*

*Twenty exponents of the New Rock 'n' Roll were fielded
by a small cartel of respectable publishers. Of these twenty
rock 'n' roll poets, nine were Oxbridge-educated. Their
ages ranged from thirty to fifty-four and, with the notable
exceptions of Simon Armitage and Carol Ann Duffy, none
had anything approaching a track record as a pop poet.*

*Had the public really embraced poetry as mass entertain-
ment for the first time in living memory? And was it true that
a new golden age of spoken word was upon us? Did this mean
that poets who performed would finally be acknowledged
by the poetry establishment? Or was it a shrewd marketing
move by a group of publishers working in tandem with the
fading Poetry Society to foist a cartload of precious sheet-
stains on to the unsuspecting public?*

*Performance poets are the Special Service wing of poetry.
Like the SAS they are more or less exempt from conventional
drilling and uniform. They take poetry to places where
poetry doesn't usually go or want to go. They work alone,
often in hostile conditions and if the mission goes wrong,
no one turns up to chopper them out of the hot spot.
Performance poets work in clubs, pubs, discos and dance
halls and keep company with rock musicians and comedians.*

*Poetry is regarded quite rightly as box-office poison.
Performance poets must therefore, in order to survive,
disguise this poison, or at least hide it in a confectionary of
rudeness and humour.*

John Cooper Clarke, Attila the Stockbroker, Joolz, Jean

*'Binta' Breeze, John Hegley, Ben Zephaniah, Linton Kwezi
Johnson, Craig Charles and several others are the people
who have wrenched poetry out of the stuffy 1970s and on to
the modern stage. They are all familiar with the empty hall,
the heckler, the shower of gob and the slung beer glass. They
are the* real rock 'n' roll *poets.*

*Most poets who have won their spurs by hijacking the
rock 'n' roll audience stayed studiously apart from the
Poetry-Is-The-New-Rock-'n'-Roll hype. And the hype stayed
away from us. Partly I suspect because they* knew *that hardly
any of the twenty new poets they were fielding would last
five minutes in a dodgy club or on a rock 'n' roll stage.*

The Independent *gave me the front page of Section Two
to vent my spleen on The Great Poetry Hype of '94. Just one
condition: I must do it in the form of an open letter. And in
verse. This poem appeared on 5 May 1994. It must have
wound someone up because part of it was read out that
morning on Radio Three.*

PS   Oh, and apparently poetry wasn't *the new rock 'n' roll
after all. Well, fancy that. Can we all get on with our gigs
now?*

What is poetry? Truth or swizz?
Shoddiest wing of Culture Biz
Poorest paid and least attended
Cinderella unbefriended
Should it scan and should it rhyme?
Sometimes maybe, but not all the time
it shouldn't.
Either way it must have soul.
Now I hear it's rock 'n' roll.

Rock 'n' roll? Rock 'n' roll?
What d'you know 'bout rock 'n' roll?
Dingy dancehall, punchy pub,
Drafty room and shabby club.
This is where the poetry goes
Keeps the art form on its toes.
Hegley, Joolz and Johnny Clarke
Ranting bravely in the dark
Rough-house venues year-on-year
Some like poetry with their beer.
Nothing like a bit of fear,
Takes the reading up a gear.

Quite apart from bookish jades
Poets come in several shades.
If the Muse is short of jobs
Sometimes she may pester yobs:
People ill-equipped to think,
Junkies, brawlers, those who drink.
After all, it's often said,
Poets are worthless till they're dead.

Now you say you've guns for hire
I'm so grateful I'm on fire.
Far be it from me to gripe,
But your perfume . . . is it Hype?
Hype – it's new from Lethargique
Hint of Po-Soc up the creek.
Years and years being out of touch.
Is it changing? No. Not much.

Ask Attila, ask Jean Breeze
Ask Ben Zephaniah – please.
Linton Kwesi Johnson too.
All know roadwork. Unlike you.
Suddenly it's rock 'n' roll.
Well, stap me. Upon my soul.
What about those gigs we did?
Don't we feature on your grid?
Must be my imagination.
Bums-on-Seats. They closed that station.
Entertainment. There. I've said it.
Nice of you to take the credit.

Poetry is rock 'n' roll
And the Muse is off the dole.
Tell the hard-pressed Lit. promoters
They'll be shifting extra quotas.
Grateful for this revelation,
They can then alert a nation
Previously happy snoring
When the poetry world was boring.

In the end I wish you luck
If the punters will have truck
With a poet centre stage
Rock 'n' Roll. It's all the rage.
As for National Poetry Day
Churlish now to stay away.
Rock 'n' roll was never fey.
Will I be there? If you pay.

The Bastard Son of J. R. Hartley

In murderous cheer
I wolf my beer
They say I'm human
Only partly.
Cold as stone
I drink alone
The bastard son of J. R. Hartley.

J. R. Hartley? I'm his kid.
Ruined my Mother's life he did.
Slimed her with his patent charm.
Wheeled genteelly on his arm
Tubbed her at the Anglers' Dance
Knew she never stood a chance.

Who's my father? Who's my father?
Grown up now and angry rather
I'll find out some way or other
Just his name. Now tell me, Mother.

First she cried and then said tartly,
'Very well . . . His name was Hartley.'
J. R. Hartley? That old sod?
Which explained the fishing rod
Smashed and broken in the attic
Somehow it was emblematic
Of a line long since gone slack.
Caught a love then threw it back.
Packed his tackle once he'd rutted.
Cleaned her out and left her gutted.

In a twilight home for ages
My poor Mother weeps and rages.
Goes downhill in steady stages.
Yellow Pages. Yellow Pages.
Yellow Pages. Yellow Pages.

We're not just there for the nice things in life.

Spot

There wasn't a lot
Came out of the spot
But was it not
The Devil's Advocaat?

Spud U Liked

Spud U liked but had 2 stop seeing 4 a while
cos it was just getting 2 heavy.

Spud U felt U could still respect in the morning.

Spud U didn't feel quite ready 2 move in with yet.

Spud U eventually settled down with.

Spud U thought was wild, crazy, Bohemian – maybe
even slightly dangerous like a unicorn seen from a
precipice. But it was back in the late 1960s, you were
both so young and it was a different time, a different
planet. And even though it was so far away down all
those long misty days, it still comes back to haunt you
from time to time and somehow U just can't seem 2
get that Spud out of your aching mind can you?? You
crazy son of a bastard. Why don't U call that Spud up
NOW??

Will You Still Love Me?

Will you still love me when I'm eighty-one?
Old and bald with a leaking bum
Clickety-clacking my dental plate
Hocking up grollies into the grate.

Will you still love me when I retire?
Coughing and farting beside the fire
Awkward as my memory fades
Blanking out entire decades.

Or will you stick me away in a home?
Catheter tube and a frame of chrome
Tumbling over twice a day
Having my food off a baby tray.

Promise me if you get concerned
To kill me when my back is turned
Club me with a baseball bat
If I ever get like that.

Darling, if you really love me,
Take me to a cliff and shove me.
In return I'll promise to . . .
Do the same if it were you.

Dead in the Barmaid's Bed

Plywood coffin draped in sacks
Funeral feast of crisps and snacks
Poor man's Prozac . . . Special Brew
Massive turn-out, guests all knew
This is what the vicar said:
'Found him dead in the barmaid's bed.'

Found him dead in the barmaid's bed
Lacy knickers on his head
What with all the gossip spread
Bound to raise his local cred.

Women tutted, men said, 'Odd.
There but for the grace of God.
Not behaviour I'd endorse . . .'
Envious as hell of course.
Seeing him in that state of grace
Hard to keep a serious face
Should have legged it – died instead
Found him dead in the barmaid's bed.

Man of Essex thoroughbred
Lead in pencil, gear in shed,
Brass in pocket, books in red,
Always kept his ferrets fed.
Found him dead in the barmaid's bed
Found him dead in the barmaid's bed
'Good owld boy,' they quietly said.
Found him dead in the barmaid's bed.

The Landlord Time Forgot

All his jokes were wartime vintage
Oft reused and in supply
Regulars would chortle at them
None of them remembered why.
Served in evenings, clad in blazer,
Food . . . 'Untouched by human hand.
Wife has cooked it. Ha ha. Geddit?
All except the greens – they're canned.'
Music? Yes, quite fond of music.
Said he liked that Scottish band.
Very Celtic. Liked the rhythm.
Simple Minds? 'No. Jimmy Shand.'

Claimed the sixties caused the problem
Sex and drugs and all that jive.
Blamed those intellectual beatniks.
Singling out the Dave Clark Five.
'That's not music. Not to my mind.
Frankly it's a bloody noise.
Got no tune. You can't enjoy it.
Hard to tell the girls from boys.
Shower of shit, this generation.
Sell their mums for half a crown.
If we had another war now –
Most of them would just lie down.

'Lager? Only keep the one on.
No room for a cooler shelf.
Wife drinks one for indigestion.
Wouldn't touch the stuff myself.
Yes, sir. Can I do you now, sir?
Just like that! What would you like?
I resemble that remark, sir!
I'm in charge! Whoops. Mind my bike!'

Welcome to Jurassic Pub.
The pies are cold. The lager's hot.
The handlebar moustache of Satan
On the landlord time forgot.

(But he never forgot time.)

First published in the Independent, *26 August 1993*

New Advice to Whirlwind Romantics

Marry in Hastings
Repent at Leicester

You've Gotta Have a Car

He couldn't get a car
Cos he didn't have a job
He couldn't take the job
Cos he didn't have a car
He couldn't date the girl
Cos he didn't have the cash
He didn't have the cash
Cos he didn't get the job
He couldn't get a date
Cos he didn't have a car
And you've gotta have a car
You've gotta have a car
You've gotta have a car.
Intcha?

He had to take a bus
Cos there wasn't any train
There wasn't any train
Cos they cut them back again
He had to take a bus
But there wasn't any back
He mightn't get a lift
And he'd have to stay the night
So because he didn't know
He decided not to go.
And you've gotta have a car
You've gotta have a car
You've gotta have a car.
Intcha?

He might have had a bike
But he didn't wanna know
And you couldn't have a bike
Cos it wasn't safe at night
And winter it was cold

And your mates'd take the piss
And you couldn't give a lift
To a *girl* or anything
Cos you've gotta have a car
You've gotta have a car
You've gotta have a car.
Intcha?

He saw a bunch of scruffs
Who were holding up the show
They were tryna stop the cars
So he went and had a go
Cos he couldn't side with *them*
So the claret had to flow
And if *they* all got their way
There'd be nothing on the road
And you'd have to take a chance
On the bus or on a train
And we'd all be back in caves
Right? 'Stead of where we are.
So you've gotta have a car
You've gotta have a car.
Intcha?

The Bicycle Ride

I'm five miles north of Shoreham, Sussex, at a place
called Upper Beeding. The temperature is high eighties,
I'm feeling slightly ill and disorientated and I recognize
that I may have bitten off more than I can chew this
time. I'm standing in a garage forecourt emptying
a bucket of cold water over my head. I'd loosely
calculated the journey as being about forty-five miles.
It will later turn out to be about fifty-eight and I hadn't
allowed for the terrible heat. There's still another eight
miles to go and it's over the South Downs.

Is there something wrong with me? My life is already
complex enough but I still feel the need sometimes
to set myself some insane task which will tax me
physically. Sunday night I had a poetry gig at the
Wedgewood Rooms in Portsmouth. Monday night
I was going to Sussex, to see Captain Sensible who
was due back from Belgium. So I'd take the train
from Essex to Liverpool Street, cycle across London
to Waterloo then take another train to Portsmouth.
After the gig I'd cycle along the coast and then wend
my way across the Downs to Chez Sensible.
   I like to cycle around England. A bicycle has an
appropriate speed and height from which to see the
place.

At 8.30 I set off from the B&B in Southsea and,
ten minutes later, I'm heading northwards out of
Portsmouth.
   Within fifteen minutes I'm in shit. The traffic is
roaring up the road towards the A27 and it's scary.
Monday morning, lots of grim faces, nasty trucks and
bad-tempered holiday-makers with cars full of whiney
kids. They're not in the mood to be courteous to a little
cyclist. The slipstream from trucks keeps knocking me

sideways, occasionally I get bipped at and sometimes someone shouts a remark out of the window at me. I'm doing nothing wrong. I'm riding a normal sit-up-and-beg bike, I'm wearing high-visibility clothing. Even my panniers, which are full of stage clothes and poetry books, have good reflectors.

The thing is that I'm not in a car. I'm not competing. I'm a bloody nuisance. I haven't paid my road tax. I shouldn't be there. Under the A27/A2030 flyover I see one or two other cyclists. They cautiously run over the road in the gaps between the cars, to get to the quieter road which leads to Chichester from Bedhampton. We're like little rodents scuttling around trying not to get crushed by the footsteps of the big bad humans.

Chichester. Bedhampton. They sound like tranquil and genteel olde-worlde English havens. The names make you think of old black-and-white films with Trevor Howard asking some wartime WAAF, 'Heppy, dahling?' You tend not to think of them being linked by nasty roaring highways full of people on the verge of road rage. What has happened to our gentle English manners? We all need to have a car and yet, judging by the looks on people's faces, it seems to be nothing but a massive arse-ache owning one. I head for Havant. I don't know anything about Havant apart from the fact that they make Tampax there. Perhaps they have an optician's shop called Eye Havant.

I make Chichester by 10.40 and stop by the canal for a cold drink and a roll-up. It's getting hot. I check tyres, nuts/bolts and map and ten minutes later I'm heading for Bognor Regis. At Bognor, I'm dangerously hot so I stick to the coast road to pick up some of the breezes. At a place called Middleton, I decide I need a soaking. Middleton-on-Sea is a very posh little place.

I go down a private-looking lane past well-appointed middle-class-type houses full of Neighbourhood Watch stickers. You know you're in the Soft South when you see those stickers. Those stickers say, 'The Underclass Stops Here . . . So keep moving, stranger.' But I don't. I find a beach. Grey stony sand and absolutely no ice-cream stalls/games/shops. Just a few people in the sea and the sound of kids playing. That curious echo that comes off a beach, like some far-off childhood memory. I have found old England at last. A nondescript, semi-deserted beach with no amenities. I tear off most of my clothes and hurl myself at the sea. I don't even have to watch my bike and bag. Who's going to come down here and pinch them? You want a semi-privatized Neighbourhood Watch beach with no amenities and a soundtrack of distant childhood memories? Come to Middleton-on-Sea. You can buy sandwiches and cola from a suspicious woman in a shop a mile up the road. Once you're decent of course.

After this highlight, the next twenty miles or so to Shoreham are a steady plod down an incredibly busy A259 coast road. The towns go by almost without me noticing. Littlehampton, Goring, West Worthing, Worthing, Lancing. Every five miles I stop at a garage and douse myself with cold water from a tap as a fore-court attendant looks worriedly on. I notice that the road menders have stopped work and are lying under trees in the early-afternoon heat. But I keep going because I don't know when I'm going to run out of push.

At Lancing I hit a genuinely cheerful working-class seafront. Loads of kids with messy ice-creams. Beach huts. Rough-looking tattoed men with sunburn. And sweaty pensioners. I stop for a cold drink, check nuts and bolts and check the map. 'Nah, mate. Yew wanna head ap froo Shorh'm. Ah far rav yew cam then? Portsm'th? Fack me!'

I'm riding along a small coastal path and I feel like Stanley asking for Livingstone when I ask a group of pensioners, 'Excuse me. But am I in Shoreham yet?'
    'No, dear. You're in Lancing but you're not far off. It's just over there. You'll see a bridge.'

At Shoreham, I turn inland and up towards the Downs. Mother nature turns up the gas. It's not just hot, it's fucking-hell hot. It's also fairly uphill. Average time for an ice-cold Coke to turn piss-warm in my drink bottle? Three minutes. And so I'm standing in this service station at Upper Beeding. And I'm feeling ill, headachey, polluted and like I've bitten off more than I could chew. This is what England's like now. The traffic makes you ill. The people outside it get poisoned and the people inside it become psychopathic. From Upper Beeding to Pycombe is about five or six miles of beautiful up-and-down country lanes. Lovely under normal circumstances but scary if the mercury's heading towards 90°F. and you feel like you're about to faint. You don't get off and walk because the breeze is the only thing that cools you down. If you stop at a road junction it's like God opened the oven door, so you keep going.
    Three miles later, after a slightly illegal half-mile along a bit of A23, I find myself in Underhill Lane. Underhill Lane is an ancient road about as wide as three horses. Featured in the Domesday Book, it was the original route which ran between the end of the forest and the beginning of the Downs. And soon after that I come upon Chez Sensible. It's 4.30 in the

afternoon. It's taken me eight hours to do fifty-eight miles. Not great by racing standards but not bad for an old pop singer with a push-bike and full panniers on this blazing hot day. The kids are playing in the yard and Rachel says, 'Oh, you made it. Miranda was worried about you. Would you like a cup of tea?'

'No, but I'd like a bucket of water,' I gasp.

And I'm looking at the map now as I write this. The whole of England was been razor-slashed by roads. So that all of these people can feel safer, faster, modern, efficient and *free* in their vehicles. You can't cycle on the blue razor-slashes. It's best not to cycle on the green razor-slashes. The red razor-slashes are not too safe and the yellow razor-slashes are more or less acceptable if no one's taking short cuts on their way home. There are little white roads as well and they're very nice but you can't go everywhere on them, because they've been carved up by the coloured roads. And I see the road protesters on TV and I think about how my parents let me cycle from Harpenden, Herts, to Putney in London when I was twelve or thirteen, almost thirty years ago. Because I wouldn't let a kid do that now. I think of the ride up through Portsmouth on Monday morning and I remember that I was genuinely scared at times. Bicycle transport is a beautiful thing. Everything about it is innocent and good. And yet car is king. It's a mad sort of tragedy, isn't it?

Wivenhoe, Essex, late August 1995

This Is What I'd Like . . . The Poet in the Pub

I'd like to be woken in the slate-grey morning by the clip-clop footsteps of a woman in heels in the street below my window and never to be absolutely sure that it wasn't a centaur with secretarial skills.

I'd like, when I get up hungover and sleep-greasy not to see the ghost in the mirror of that pale boy with guitars in his eyes. Not to feel sad or to regret and not to hear madness tapping at the bathroom window or scratching and giggling at the back door downstairs.

I'd like to be telephoned by George Martin after breakfast to be told he's fixed the time machine at last, it's 1966 and can I please get myself over to Abbey Road because the Beatles can't finish the *Revolver* LP with *my* help.

I'd like lunch with Dusty Springfield, tea with Julie Christie and dinner with Henry's Cat.

I'd like real ale. But what I'd really prefer would be fantasy ale where, after a few pints, society devolves into lots of small, self-policing village units and nobody's ever homeless or hungry.

I'd like it if when you said, 'Let's be seeing those glasses off, please', that the whole pub trooped down to the railway station and tearfully put their glasses on the London train while a brass band played 'Goodbye, Dolly Gray'.

I'd like a packet of crisps. Neglected Orchard flavour. Autumn Churchyard. Smoked Politician. Crunchy Monarchist.

I'd like a whole rainy weekend of pills and gin listening to old Ronettes records and bitching.

I'd like to be with a weird creature, dancing on the shingle at Aldeburgh, at midnight when the stars burn holes in the showbiz sky like a million cheap cigarettes.

I'd like it if that boring bastard who's always talking about his money had a surprise birthday visit from the Demented Alsatian-O-Gram people, whereby, at an appointed time, two brawny black-hooded figures, dressed like medieval executioners, would burst into the pub, hold him over the counter and sing 'Happy Birthday', while a large demented alsatian gave him a bloody good seeing to.

I'd like the following choices on the jukebox: High winds in tall trees. Waves crashing on rocks. Crows cawing in winter fields, Seagulls following ploughmen. Then, after that, Small Faces singles, A-sides and B-sides, all night long.

I'd like that private function you've got booked upstairs on Saturday *not* to be Darren's and Mandy's engagement party, followed by a disco and punch-up with all the girls crying, 'Aoow naoow! Leave 'im alone, Tony!' I'd like it to be the site that Marvin Gaye chose for his resurrection gig with Jimi Hendrix.

I'd like the men's toilet to have potted plants, a string quartet and a life-size wax model of Isadora Duncan holding the soap. I'd like the garden to have all the homeless giraffes from London Zoo and I'd like more ghosts in the cellar, please.

I'd like Death to turn up in a Citroën 2CV wearing
a stripey blazer and a boater hat, then go away again
because he got the date of the Trad Jazz night wrong.

I'd like it if you had Alien Access for the terrestrially
challenged. For instance: Do you have any landing
lights on the roof? Is there a sign outside saying,
SATURNIAN COACH PARTIES WELCOME? How
is an alien craft supposed to know you're here?

And I'd like you to think about all of this, because this
is what I'd like.

Oh, all right then. A pint of Heineken and some change
for the cigarette machine, please.

His Majesty the Dog

His majesty the dog
Expects a royal pardon
At 6 a.m. on Sunday
He needs to use your garden
Despite the fact you're wheezing
You're naked and it's freezing
Don't press him for a reason
It's tantamount to treason.

His majesty the dog
Though you may think him rude
Demands your prompt attention
Regarding any food
He shouldn't have to wait
At risk of seeming crude
His nose is in your plate
For he dwells among the great.

His majesty the bloody dog
Would like to make a racket
At any time he pleases
And you'll just have to hack it.
His majesty the stupid mutt
Will treat you like a dipstick
And quietly commandeer your chair
To sit and lick his lipstick.

His majesty the filthy sod
Who's costly as he's useless
Reserves the right to mount your friends
And splash them with his juices.
His majesty the flyblown twat
May use your house and soil it
And take refreshment any time
By drinking from your toilet.

His majesty the scumbag
Who's great as he is good
Requests these daily pleasures:
A ramble in the wood
A roll in something nasty
A munch on something dead
And then he can anoint you
While joining you in bed.

His majesty the bastard
Will grant no absolution
The sin of not being canine
Means moral destitution
And should you overlook this
He'll reinforce the warning
By pissing on your bedspread
At seven in the morning.
His majesty the furry lump
Can almost make you weep
But you'd cry for fucking hours
If the sod got put to sleep.

Ode to a Jerusalem Artichoke

In April 1993 and January 1994, I appeared in an upmarket gardening programme on Channel 4, called Grow Your Greens. *This programme temporarily eclipsed any worth I previously had as a poet or musician. The following poem was commissioned for the programme but, for reasons of time, was neved used.*

The artichoke (Jerusalem)
Or Helianthus Tuberosus
Though delicious
Can be vicious
If consumed in larger doses
Do beware
Of surplus air
You of weaker constitutions
Artichokes can be volcanic
Novice diners often panic
Not so much effluvium
Closer to Vesuvium
Do excuse me
Beg your pardon
May I venture to your garden?
Please direct me
Without fail
Thought I heard a nightingale
Noxious gases rising high
In the darkening winter sky
Hope to God they won't blame me
When the bird falls from the tree
Blame the soup
Or blame the chef
Hope the other guests are deaf
When pronouncing artichoke
Do it with a silent F.

Inge

She was quietly radioactive
In a crowd of dull earthlings
Her almond eyes were the pale light
Of churchyard moons after storms
When the sky is like petrol in a puddle.
And her dress was cheap and raggy
And hung on her long-boned frame
Like a dead dancing partner at dawn
And she looked so good in a way
That women of a certain atmosphere . . .
Will always make rags look good
And all these thoughts came to mind
Of observatories high and lonely
In the starry wooded hills of summer
Of flying saucers over space-age cities
Of transmissions from the high blue stars
And of impossible travel faster than light.
Well, this is how she was.
And her name was Inge.

About Twenty-seven Definitions of Love

As a chimera – a vain and idle fancy.

A unicorn caught briefly and let go.

As a mental illness. Stark obsessed and silent.

Forbidden by parents but continued secretly anyway.

Separated by authorities and gaoled but defiantly
scrawling its name on cell walls.

The smell of perfume on a shopgirl's hair reminding
an old man of his dead wife.

As a slow-motion car crash in an unsuspecting
traveller's life.

A postmistress, with her mind on half-day closing,
wakes suddenly and licenses her lover's vehicle.

Under the clock at Waterloo Station, giving it one more
five minutes before catching an empty train home to
Guildford.

Crushed like chestnut leaves on a wet pavement after
shopping on Saturday.

The score of nothing at tennis. But everything to you.

In an office, half asleep at its desk, dreaming
impossible weekends.

The windy airport tarmac between a returning war
veteran and his headscarfed wife.

Eked out in cross-Atlantic letters twice a week for thirty-seven years until one day a letter doesn't come.

In stilettos and black nail varnish, dancing round its handbag in a disco until a boy plucks up courage.

Lordly leftovers given to a pale delivery boy by a kindly under house parlourmaid.

A WAAF reapplying lipstick in a jeep and hoping that the Lancaster bomber makes it back again.

A strong young man pushing his friend in a wheelchair through the park in March before taking him back to the clinic.

A senior policewoman unexpectedly pregnant at forty-three by a probation officer ten years younger.

A female student unhappy after mucking up her exams over a married lecturer who promised to call and never did.

Slowly dawning on two people whose dreadful partners ran off with each other.

Someone you'd known all these years and never thought . . .

The song you always hated on the radio which you now realize was especially written as the soundtrack to what you're going through.

You keep checking in the mirror to see if you've changed into somebody else. Somebody better.

When friends say, 'For chrissakes, you two. Leave each other alone for five minutes, will you?'

Deserted, drunk and raving in a crumbling tower by a lake in winter.

Haunting noblemen's follies, cafés, parks, streets, corridors and empty houses where it once walked in delirium.

You who are currently in love will know I am telling the truth.

The Tokyo Duck Patrol

In September 1994 I went to Japan for the second time that year. On this occasion it was a rock tour to promote a CD. This tour diary was first published in the Independent *on 29 September 1994.*

Our two minibuses have been stuck in a traffic jam on the Rainbow Bridge for almost an hour. It's a sweaty 92°F., we've had a twelve-hour flight and this is Friday night in Tokyo. Tired? Hot? Aching for a beer? Feel you deserve something better in life? Then you must be Martin Newell at the beginning of a Japanese tour.

In minibus No. 1 are Kevin, Tiv, Garrie Dreadful and myself (smoking). In No. 2 are Captain Sensible, XTC's Dave Gregory and New Model Army's Nelson (non-smoking). Tokyo is a forty-mile sprawl of *Bladerunner* modernity. It has a population of about 11 million, most of whom are sitting in their cars in an apparent attempt to prevent us from reaching our hotel.

We are extremely well looked after. Out hosts leave nothing to chance. In spite of this, Sensible still wanders out five minutes before pick-up time to graze at pavement noodle booths. Captain Sensible is one of life's strays. He gets to a foreign country, buys himself a bus and tube map and goes native. He often returns wearing strange clothes and smelling of exotic food.

We are to play our first two gigs at On Air West in Tokyo. The airline that flew us out here actually lost our guitars and stage bags in Paris. They eventually turned up at the hotel two hours before our first promotion. Dave Gregory snarled, 'This won't be anything to do with the Japanese. This'll be the bloody French.' Dave is the quietest member of Newell's all-

singing, all-dancing alien all-stars. This is why I was
surprised to see him being followed down the street by
nine adoring female fans. I gather this doesn't occur
when he's at home in Swindon.

People back home tend not to believe these stories but
it is absolutely true that English pop musicians in early
middle years can still get mobbed by female fans in
Tokyo. It's very polite mobbing but it is still mobbing.
So there. It might be more fun if it all wasn't so terribly
and tragically late.

Captain's small flotilla of fans are nicknamed 'Duck
Patrol'. This is because Captain has taught them all
to make quacking noises as he leads them in a clumsy
twist routine in hotel foyers. No, we don't understand
it either.

By the end of the first gig our 'crack fighting unit' has
become a bunch of pantomime dames. Sensible does his
favourite trick of falling over mid-solo then dragging
the hapless Japanese roadie into a tangle of leads and
mike stands. By second night at On Air West, Captain
and I are wearing mascara, lipstick and beauty spots.
Tiv is wearing a pink acrylic glam-rock wig and Nelson
still looks like he's playing in New Model Army.

Dave Gregory leads the band onstage to the strains
of Jack Payne and the BBC Dance Orchestra singing
'Make Yourself a Happiness Pie'. We go offstage with
a stupid walk, then come back for an encore with a
pop standard which we haven't rehearsed. Sometimes
we're lucky. The Japanese seem to like it.

Later in the week we take the Bullet Train south to

Osaka. At average speeds of 180 m.p.h., it's the fastest train in the world. It's so quiet, you can speak in a whisper, which is what I'm reduced to doing, as my voice is on the blink. I gargle with lemon water and drink plenty of fluids. I pray this will work because the alternatives are the Illegal French Throat Spray (which is dangerous) or the dreaded raw onion marinaded in raw sugar, which can give you nuclear flatulence.

Back in Tokyo, Dave's fans have clubbed together and bought him a twentieth-anniversary Fender Strat. British customs will later charge him £95 in tax to bring it into the UK. Wonderful, isn't it?

At Narita Airport, days later, Dave's fan club and a rather tearful Duck Patrol are already here to take photos of us and wave us off. Kevin comes back from the ticket desk. The good news? Because the airline lost our guitars earlier, we've had out tickets upgraded to Club Class. The bad news? We stop for refuelling in Moscow and change back to an airbus from Paris. At Heathrow I feel absolutely tip-top on Garrie Dreadful's 'Smoke and Drink Your Way to Health' method. I'm to spend the subsequent thirty-six hours regretting this.

Cupid's Toothpaste

Cupid's toothpaste on my duvet
Aphrodite's Evostick
Oozing from the cleft of Venus
Salty-sweet and honey thick
Where the wand of love was sick.

Cupid's toothpaste on the mouthpiece
Of the blue-veined beef bassoon
Seasick in Apollo's cavern
Underneath the buttock moon.
Only you can play this tune.

The Railway Children

I became obsessed
With this film
The Railway Children.
I saw it fifty-two times.
After a while . . .
I got a peaked cap
And took to
Waving at trains.
Every day I went.
And I waved.
Until one day
Not only
Did Jenny Agutter
Fail to turn up.
Again.
But some rough men
In orange jackets
Gave me a severe beating.

goodbye.

The Dignity of Labourers

Ah bin fuckin' workin'
Then ah went fuckin' drinkin'
And cos it's fuckin' Friday
Ah've bin fuckin' thinkin'
Ah'll take you out t'night.
All right?

Ah got some fuckin' money
So it's my fuckin' treat
Ah'm really fuckin' starvin'
Ah've had fuck all to eat.
Bin in the fuckin' pub.
Give my back a scrub?

Ah really fuckin' missed you.
Ah thought of you at night.
I wanna fuckin' see you
In the fuckin' light.
Oi. That's not the soap.
Any fuckin' dope?

Because yore fuckin' clever
Because yore fuckin' sweet
Because yore not some fuckin' bim
Ah dragged up off the street
Ah'll stay in if you want to.
D'you want to?

Because ah fuckin' love you
Ah'm yores fer fuckin' takin'
But take it fuckin' easy
Ah'm really fuckin' achin'
My knee is fuckin' murder.
Ah bashed it on a girder.

The job is fuckin' crazy
It's doin' me fuckin' head in
Ah'm gunna fuckin' jack it in
And wear out all yore beddin'
In smashed, unwedded bliss.
Oi . . . Gis a fuckin' kiss.

Milk

It was clotted
Off-white
It didn't smell quite . . .
Right.
It was
Semi-skilled milk.

Wild Crazy Chick

She was this wild crazy chick.
She'd drifted up from the south coast
That sultry summer.
She liked me to run naked
Around her room
While she threw tennis balls at me
Coated in garlic mayonnaise
And sex was always really violent
But fantastic.
They moved me to another area after that.
My parents didn't think
It was any kind of a relationship
For twelve-year-old boy
To have with his grandmother.

The English Are a Nation of Bass Guitarists

The English are a nation of bass guitarists. Our pop musicians and football hooligans are internationally famous. And yet at home we sit glazed in badly furnished bars and practice mediocrities on each other.

Our old with their watery blue eyes dreaming of forgotten fairground rudenesses. Safe in their allotment sheds, they use dark forces: high on Wincarnis and Victory-V lozenges they evoke the demon Formby, the jackal-headed Gracie Fields and, worst of all, the Rhinestone Christian Elvis whose form materializes from a chipped Coronation mug. Nights draw in and the bonfire is lit with pre-Wilson-government copies of the *Daily Express* and Esso Blue paraffin. A parallel world exists within these sheds where Suez is retrieved, Hanratty dies tomorrow and the barbershops are smoky, damp and full on a Friday night. Mentally birching foul-mouthed boys and summarily stringing up queers, they daily repatriate Mr Patel at the corner shop before turning the mud-cooled Vickers gun on hordes of imaginary fuzzy-wuzzies approaching from the west. And then they totter home on Stilton legs to walk their overfed and pile-ridden dogs.

Chin up. Best foot forward. Nose to the grindstone. Shoulder to the wheel. Do them all at once. Bloody uncomfortable, isn't it? We didn't have teenagers when I was young. There was a war to be fought. You see these fields? They were all fields when I was a boy.

The English are a nation of eccentrics. Hardly. Eccentricity is conferred only when accompanied by age, wealth or title. Preferably all three. In other circumstances the English firmly attempt to mallet their colourful young into a tight barrel of conformity. And what do the young do? They become bass guitarists. It eases the hurtle through the gauntlet of the fashion nazis to be able to say, 'Yes. I'm in a band.' Or, 'Yes. I used to be in a band.' And what did you play? The bass guitar? Oh, really? So did I. Well, there you go.

You don't believe me? Go on then. Walk into a pub full of young people and say, 'Hands up all bass guitarists.' See how many you get.

After they've played the bass guitar for a while, they get jobs or sometimes join the Labour Party. Welcome to the concerned classes – you've graduated. If that waggish demented poet drives to your house at midnight in a dumper truck and proceeds to pitchfork the lorryload of gassed Kurdish children on to your organic camomile lawn, you have every right to complain.
    You've done your bit. You played the bass guitar.
    Don't cry or remark what a singularly beautiful people the Kurdish are. Say, 'I used to be a bass guitarist and I'm calling the police.'

Now what of my English mother and her activities with the British Legion and ATS old girls. Do they use dark forces? Highly likely. Best not to dwell on that but to remember instead how she picked pieces of diced carrot out of the telephone dial with a geometry compass at 4 a.m. after my drunken brother had thrown up through the serving hatch into the kitchen.

But my mother with her cupcakes and *Woman's Realm* recipes was Bride of Satan and I survive only to impart this to you: The English are a nation of bass guitarists. Beware the quiet ego of the quiet bass-player. Beware his quietly superior girlfriend with her beatific smile, infuriating laugh, traveller chic and lotus position as she tells you, 'Oh, Richard's really really wise, you know? He doesn't say much, but when he does . . .' It's entirely predictable.

So where does this discreet wock and woll webellion start? In a secondhand shop as a rule. Money changes hands and the secondhand bass is pulled from the window as if it were Excalibur being drawn from a stone.

And where does it end? In a series of benefit gigs run by compassionate greybeards who all used to play bass guitars themselves. These worthies know all about the old men using dark forces in their allotment sheds. They are well versed in their methods and will counsel you if you wish.

So if the beautiful ghosts of the dead Kurdish children ever come to haunt you, each greybeard will know how to help you. The bass guitar. Reassuring now with its rusty strings, it nestles among your Paul Simon LPs like a spiritual Kalashnikov. It waits only for that doubting moment when you turn like a faltering bride to your handsome groom Normality and say, 'I do.'